Day Trading

A quick beginner guide

By

Richard Smiths

Table of Contents

Introduction

I want to thank you and congratulate you for downloading the book, Day Trading. This book contains proven steps and strategies on how to earn money in Day Trading. I am truly convinced that I am able to provide you with the value and information that you are looking for.

In this eBook, I am going to present you all the information you need to possess if you plan to get into this business. My focus will be on showing you what are the day trading basics, as well as all the things you definitely need to know before you get into this business.

There are so many trading books out there on the market that is simply made up of ideas that can be easily found on the Internet for free, and this book is not one of them. This book is not another "Day Trading for

Dummies" type of book but contains real strategies and solid school of thoughts of accomplished day traders. It is a no-nonsense, honest guide to successful day trading that I believe anyone can learn from.

Day trading can definitely be simple, but please, do not make the mistake of thinking it is easy. It is very far from that.

I know that you probably heard many people saying "Day trading is easy" and I know you saw plenty of websites telling you how you can achieve success in day trading after reading a couple of pages or attending some stupid online class. I would definitely like if this was true and that, magically, you can become a successful trader overnight.

Please, do not be fooled with this. Like in every profession on the world, you are going to need much more than attending a class or reading an eBook in order to become a master at something. You need a solid education, a good plan and some experience.

You will get exact and reliable information in regards to the topic and issue covered. The book is sold with the information that the publisher is not necessary to render accounting, officially acceptable, or otherwise, professional services. If information is necessary, legal or acceptable, an experienced individual in the profession should be ordered.

Thanks again for downloading this book, I hope you enjoy it!

Chapter 1 What is Day trading

Day trading is defined as "the buying and selling of securities on the SAME day". It is usually done online and in hopes of taking advantage of and reaping benefits from small, short-term price fluctuations.

Here is an example: You could buy 1000 shares of Amazon stocks at 10:15 AM at let's say - $425 per share. 10 minutes later it rises to $426, you made $1 per share. Since you have bought 1000 shares, you just earned yourself $1000 in profit (minus a small commission for the brokerage). This potential to make that kind of money in such a short period of time is what attracts people to day trading. It is not uncommon to make $300 in 30 minutes, $600 in 20 minutes, or $1500 in 5 minutes, and so on.

it is not always this simple. I know plenty of people and websites are selling you the idea that you can get rich overnight by trading stocks. It's not necessarily impossible, but it's rather unrealistic.

However, you can make a lot of money if you possess certain tools and know special strategies. As with any profession, if you want success, you need a PLAN! Without a plan, you are wasting time, and even worse, you are wasting money.

I will try to show you all the mistakes you need to avoid, as well as some of my best strategies that can be useful. If you are determined and committed, I am convinced you can accomplish anything you put your mind on.

However, day trading is not for everyone. If you are not good at facing losses, I recommend you NOT to go into this field of business.

The cold hard truth is: over 90% of traders make a loss in trading. Many of them gave up before they give themselves the chance to make a profit.

Why do most day traders fail?

That is a common question for a people, so quite a few came and thus many was unable. The staggering percentage folks who failed presented rise for the opinion of which trading can be mysterious, as well as even a tremendous scam of which profits just the loaded and effective.

Now, there are many reasons the reason people fail with this business. The 2 major main reasons why day traders lose money consistently could be because of their lack of knowledge in regards to the notion regarding "risk vs reward" along with their lack of discipline. A trader can enter a trade wanting to make $1 per share, however if his or her potential risk is $2, it's not necessarily worth using the buy and sell. Many usually are so blinded through the reward that they can fail to produce a well-formed strategy before getting in. This kind of, in convert, leads for the second cause, which can be discipline. I firmly think that the math concepts of trading is extremely straightforward along with easy. It is a person's emotion that always screws the game. Being unsure of when in order to cut burning, being stubborn on the losing buy and sell and revenge trading the stock they have got just shed money about are a few examples regarding ill-disciplined trading. These dealers ultimately fail and maybe they are not who you wish to be.

Many people have shed their personal savings on stock investing and for that reason, trading can often be seen for evil. Day trading investing is often synonymous having gambling along with betting, but in the event you take time to learn along with appreciate the marketplace, you will realize that day trading is vastly different from your standard gambling.

Chapter 2   Why you should start day trading

Here are some reasons why I believe day trading is the actual path to wealth.

One, the money. That's obvious; I mean that's probably why you are reading this book in the first place.

Two, location independence: you can do day trading anywhere in the world where there is an internet connection. If you choose to sit at home, at a café, or at the pool or beach (as long as there is Wi-Fi), you're good.

Three, you can make your own hours. If you choose to work just one hour a day, that's fine. If you want to work less or more, that's fine, too. Whatever works for you?

Four, your race does not matter, your looks do not matter, and your social status does not matter. You also don't need a college degree, even though knowledge or an economic background obviously doesn't hurt, but no expensive 4-year degree or more is required. None of these things are important. You only need to have sufficient funds to trade.

Other than that, there are so many differences between day trading and all the other businesses. You do not have to hire anyone; you do not have to have employees and manage your business, you do not have to worry about their performances etc.. You do not have to rent office space or to worry about customers, invoices, equipment.

These are all the reasons why day trading should be your next big thing. If you are motivated and determined, then there is no excuse not to start earning money with day trading even today. Later in this eBook, I will show you some of the possible earning as well, which will motivate you even more. Anyway, let's stick to the basics for now.

The following are some of the major reasons why you should start day trading:

1) Reduced capital investment

Like a most businesses, you don't need lots of money to start day trading investing. In the

United states, you need almost $1000 to start day trading investing in the foreign currency market and just regarding $25, 000 to get started on day trading throughout stocks. This is somewhat amount money considering the leverage you get and the amount of profits you can rip from your trading.

2) The particular Returns are quick

If you want a profitable business with instantaneous benefits, then day exchanging is that business. In day exchanging, you buy and also sell financial instruments on the same day. This simply means that you begin counting your profits some hours or even units after entering a new trade. You may also convert your profits into cash promptly. You can reinvest your wages and make far more profits. This makes this a wonderful business for someone who would like to make money more quickly.

3) No need to hire worker

If what can be keeping you from starting a profitable business is the stress of suffering employees then day trading investing is list of positive actions. In day exchanging, you don't need to hire employees that you can comfortably do it on your own. All you need is usually a trading account, a few devices and your ventures.

4) It costs less to own

The total cost of accomplishing day trading is quite minimal. Other than your investment all other things you need are much less expensive costly than running the original business. The commission per trade is quite minimal and sometimes you will need to pay less than $10. You don't need an place of work, inventory, and machinery which often further reduces the price tag on starting and running your work time trading business. Other issues that is included in traditional office business including insurance, goods shipping and delivery and handling, displays and promotions and others don't apply. The fact that you don't handle customers directly means that you don't ought to spend more in running your work day trading business. Furthermore, you save considerable time as you don't ought to handle invoices, companies and customer products and services activities.

5) It gives equal opportunity for earning

Unlike a normal day job where there's discrepancies in earning depending on educational background, career title, race and in some cases gender, there isn't such a part of day trading. All you want to earn is usually a solid plan and also good judgment. If you have for a while been thinking involving economic activity to undertake that doesn't come with the usual discrimination issues in the day job, then consider day trading investing. Sometimes you can be discriminated against depending on your color as well as past history from the traditional business or when searching for work. There isn't such discrimination in day trading investing.

6) It put in at home to learn and also manage

Day trading is usually a simple art to know. All you need to learn is the standard. Once you grasp them, you can start trading. Since all you could do in a new trade is keep an eye on the entry along with the exit, day trading is quite easy to learn and manage. And can truly take you just a couple of hours each day for making lots of profits.

Chapter 3   How to get started

To many people new professionals, these are the most important issues. "What should it take to get started? What broker must i choose? Must i need any supercomputer? " My partner and i don't feel that answers to any of these issues will assist you to become a successful trader overnight.

If an individual ever considered getting into ecommerce, then I'm able to guess you might have strong motivation and definately will to come to be rich. As you know, being motivated being rich is actually saying, "You are already ". On the other hand, you do not desire to be rich, rely on me. You would like to be wealthy!

As many individuals are not aware of the variation between "rich" as well as "wealthy", Let me show you the principle difference.

• Being rich" means you might have fortune (which doesn't mean you might have earned them).

- "Being wealthy" indicates that you've time to savor money you might have earned and time for it to do what for you to do.

In my opinion, there usually are three strategies to become wealthy:

- Start your own personal company or your own personal internet small business

- Invest into real-estate

- Start a profession in trading!

Obviously, the very first two usually are much harder and much more complicated. I am going to explain an individual why. To get started on your very own company and possess a profitable online business, you are going to need to make your very own product, market place your product or service, find clients, sell these individuals your product or service, and for the end, accumulate the payments.

Successful trading stems from good habits and discipline, and they are not skills that you can acquire in a short time of moment. With that said, you do have to spend some time thinking about how much you are prepared to risk as well as which brokers are made for you to help you trade of your means as well as without too much stress.

How Much Money Do I Need To Start?

I hope you might be interested to find about how much cash you actually want to get started in order to day business.

Unfortunately for many that actually want to participate inside high regular trading, there is something called the 25k rule in the usa. This rule states you need to maintain no less than at the very least $25, 000 within your account constantly. This will be the minimum amount the SEC requires proper who wants to make 4 and up trades for each 5 morning period. That means once your account balance would drop because of $24, 999, the rule kicks in therefore you would only be permitted to trade 3 x per 5 morning period, which in turn obviously prevents you through actual day trading. So retain this planned.

You have to know that there exists emotion involved during trading that may never end up being fully experienced by simply paper exchanging. In various other words, you may not take papers trading severely because no real money is involved. Before you put in place any number of real cash, always select the thought preparation that you can lose the whole thing. I realize that this could be difficult to understand just through words, because a person actually dealing with it. I generally recommend people to print or take note of their principles of trading using a Post-It and place it on your keyboard where you can see the item during exchanging. This can always serve as being a reminder to keep your awesome during exchanging hours and not bust your account in a moment connected with folly.

Equipment: What Is Needed In Order To Trade Successfully?

Hmm, let's see. Oh, how can I forget that? You are probably willing to know what else, except money, you are going to need if you decide to get into this business.

Well, here is a short list and I am going to devote couple of paragraphs for each one of them.

1. A computer

2. An internet connection

3. A broker

4. Good strategy

5. Charting software

As you can see, these are five must haves for this business. You will never achieve success in day trading if you miss some of these.

When talking about a computer, I wanted you to let you know that you do not need the latest technology. Most of the charting software is compatible with old technology and they always work perfectly on Windows (my recommendation) so I advise you not to spend big amounts of money. What I would do is I would purchase a second screen so you can have charting software on one screen and trading platform on the second one.

Reliable internet connection is must. Never cheapen here.

BROKERS

When you would like a dealer, you have to find the one that serves the needs you have.

Understand in which brokers won't make or even break your trading; it is yourself in which dictates this specific. However, a great broker will make your lifestyle easier and let you be more centered on the day trading as an alternative to worrying about stuffs that are significantly less important.

In other words, a beneficial broker is the one that complements your trading technique. If you get you have greater success stock trading on your short part, you desire to find brokers which have good borrows regarding shares to short, permitting you to short a greater variety involving stocks. You may determine your style of exchanging from activities in cardstock trading. If you prefer to trade large quantities (>10000) involving low-priced stocks, you would want to find a dealer that charges commission over a per business basis. A per share foundation commission will likely be way too costly for an individual. The key to the present is to discover the broker in which suits your style of trading probably the most. Personally, I also like broker agents with excellent customer satisfaction because often during the trading hrs, you need a response to problems fast and also a great broker customer satisfaction that will be easily reachable will go further in providing you a more pleasant trading experience with a lesser amount of headaches. This is the list involving brokers, i have personally used, before few a long time and my overview of them:

Sure Trader

Pros: No PDT rule, you can open an account for as little as $500.Allows international traders to day trade US stock markets. Decent shares to borrow. Low commission at $5 trade per 10000 shares.

Cons: Very poor customer service. Slow response time and poor grasp of English. They are also based in Bahamas and are therefore less transparent.

Recommendation: I will say if you are starting off with a small account and wish to avoid the PDT, this is your only option. Both their trading platform and customer service are hit and miss cases.

Center point Securities

Pros: Excellent customer service and wide ranges of shares available to short. They use Sterling Pro platform that is one of the best out there. Overall, a very high quality product.

Cons: You will require at least $50,000 to open an account.

Recommendation: I highly recommend Center point Securities IF you are thinking about going in fulltime with more than $50,000 to spare and already have some experience in trading.

Interactive Broker

Pros: 2 tiers of structure that caters to both frequency traders and high volume traders. Has one of the lowest commissions in the industry. Very wide range of investment vehicles.

Cons: $10,000 initial sum required. Sub-par customer service. Average borrow list.

Recommendation: IB is a decent broker from my experience. But lately, I have not been trading on it unless I need to locate more shares to short.

Speed Trader

Pros: 10,000 symbol short list and has good locates for stocks you want to short. $0.001 per share in commission. ECN fee rebates.

Cons: Mobile trading only available to iOS products.

Recommendation: I will recommend Speed Trader because of their highly negotiable commission structure which may allow a trader to pay as low as $1 per trade as well as their robust shares to short list.

Charting software

It is also necessary, of course. I am not going to spend too many words on this. There is a lot of quality information on the Internet, which can give you a review of all charting software and provide you with all the features.

Last but not least, a trading strategy. You can have the best computer, best internet connection, most experienced broker, best software and an account with huge balance, but if you do not have a trading strategy, you are only going to lose money. So, you should be aware all of this trading strategy.

Fancy Trading Terms Simplified

So before we get into more detail talking about stocks, forex, etc. let's look at a couple of essential terms that you will hear pretty much all the time when getting into day trading or stock investing in general.

Capital requirements pretty much refers to how much money you need in order to invest. Your capital investment will vary depending on if you are using stocks, options or futures. Options, for example, are cheaper than stocks but carry more value (but also more risk).

Leverage is basically how much benefit you receive out of something in relation to how much you initially put in. For example, while you can make a lot of money off of futures, you actually don't have to put in or spend that much when buying them. High leverage is awesome but also usually means the possibility of losing a lot, it all and sometimes even more than you have.

Volatility basically means fluctuation. If one says, "the market is very volatile right now", it means there are a lot changes in price movement in a short period of time, in other words, lots of ups and downs at this moment. This is usually good for us day traders since we can take advantage of this situation as prices fluctuate.

Liquidity refers to the degree of availability of an asset. Cash, for example, is highly liquid while real estate is not. You can trade cash immediately, while it takes a while until you actually sell (liquidate) a property.

Then there are also the two essential terms "going long" as well as "going short".

Going "long" means buying and speculating that the price of something will go up. This is your standard trade. You buy a stock for $50 and hope it will go up to $60, once it gets up to $60, you sell it. You took a "long" position.

However, when you go "short", you actually bet against that stock. You are speculating that this particular stock will decrease in value. Professional traders often use this strategy when they feel like a stock cannot rise more than it has already done. The concept is easy in essence and much benefit can be derived from this when one has enough experience. Going short can be awesome but you can also shoot yourself in the foot with this.

Chapter 4   Building a Watch list

Carrying out homework is important to per day trader. A smart trader the moment related learning how to trade to help taking examinations in college. He used to take any statistics course in school and it also was a few days before the ultimate paper. Everybody was permitted to bring within the A4 sized piece of paper to write all your formulae or comments about it and bring into the exam area. It was such as a cheat page of sorts. He didn't organize the quiz but he squeezed hold of any photocopied version with the cheat sheet with the smartest college student in course. Armed your genius good article, he went directly into take your exam. But in the exam, he can't do a single question. He didn't produce the be unfaithful sheet, and he or she didn't learn how to use it at all. He didn't learn how to apply any formula as well as spent quite a while just to get where an item of information was written. He didn't go through the process connected with understanding why certain things were prepared down as well as certain things weren't. Only the person who personally wrote it will understand and they're the style of people who flourish in your exam. The identical logic relates to trading. If you only blindly make use of somebody's strategies watching lists as well as hope you can replicate his or her success, you will be in to get a rude shock in the actual investing. You must understand the rationale behind just about every move as well as ultimately, you wish to create your own plan that works by yourself. In this particular chapter, I can explain on ways to form ones watch record and with any luck ,, you can understand some of the thought method that passes through my head when i find stocks and options to industry.

Every day, you need to enter this market with any clean slate and a well-formed approach. The best time and energy to formulate this course of action is accomplishing research within the night before. The marketplace closes from the afternoon therefore you always expand the pattern of getting an hour or so at night to review your trades during the day. This means that you can get better and better over time.

A excellent portion of times should also be used to creating your watch list. A watch list contains a listing of stock that you just will probably want to play tomorrow depending on your screening criteria. Usually, you create a listing of not greater than 10 stocks on the list the night before. Next morning prior to market unwraps, you will have to review this particular list as well as update it in line with the pre-market action with the stocks. you possibly can either sign up for those which can be not trading as outlined by your approach or add more tickers who're setting up nicely through pre-market.

If you would like to trade NASDAQ listed stocks and selective NYSE stocks; you hardly ever touch OTCBB or pink sheet stocks due to the lack of volume and liquidity. You can trade using the one-minute candlestick chart and do not use any fancy indicators such as the MACD or the RSI. It is my philosophy to keep things clear and easy. NASDAQ provides the greatest liquidity and you can move in and out of the market relatively easy. To the surprise of many, you like to keep your stock screening process really,

REALLY simple. You can use 4 main indicators to determine if a stock can be traded.

1) Volume

2) Range

3) Support/Resistance

4) Chart Pattern

VOLUME

I look for charts that are in play with tons of volume. You want a large audience to be following the chart, because this way, support and resistance lines will become a self-fulfilling prophecy. Typically, a chart should have at least 1,000,000 daily shares traded for me to consider it. The volume should also have seen a spike in comparison with the past daily volume of the stock.

RANGE

The next criteria is range, I look for a stock that has at least 0.25 cents in range. Anything less than that is not worth the time because of how little the stock moves every day. Penny stocks are a different matter because of their low stock price. A large range indicates to a trader that it is volatile and he can make a larger amount of money per share traded.

SUPPORT AND RESISTANCE

With regards to using complex analysis, I really do not more than complicate matters. You probably have learnt coming from other buying and selling books about using fancy indicators including moving averages as well as Donchian routes. I don't use these. The simply indicators you may use for stock investing are service and level of resistance lines. If you locate that particular indicators are most often working well in your case already, then that is great. Stick with the information you are aware of and what may seem to work by yourself.

Support along with resistance lines have become important to determine if the stock can be traded. If your stock tries go higher and pauses past an argument of level of resistance, there might be a surge with volume due to the fact everybody believes the stock could surge that is certainly when this stock starts to pattern upwards. Nonetheless, it is not always the way it is. There can be cases associated with fake outbreaks or breakdowns that capture people into convinced that the investment can trend within the anticipated path. Eventually, in the event the stock chart won't move not surprisingly, these men and women panic along with the stock may well spike within the opposite path. It is essential to get a plan in the event they occur. Once the breakout on a long information happened, I like to buy on the pull returning or because the chart dips.

Entries have become important into a day trader when just about every tick matters. I don't choose to chase the stock if it's at the highs when you never know when a chart may possibly pull returning and freeze. Even though, eventually, it may possibly rise back and you will be accurate, you save the throbbing headache of seeing the information going against you.

HOW TO USE THE WATCHLIST

The Watch list is created so that you can have a better feel of the momentum of the stocks you want to trade on the next day. If you already have a Watchlist written out, you save yourself the panic of looking through a whole list of stocks again. In the next morning after you have compiled your Watchlist, you want to be looking at these stocks and look out for a confirmation of your trade idea. Is the stock moving in the direction as you anticipated it to be? Is a trend forming in your desired direction? If the stock is not moving how you think it should be, take it off your immediate Watchlist at market open and allow the stock to set up throughout the trading day first. This way, you are actually narrowing down your Watchlist to a few stocks that you are most confident about playing at the market open.

Chapter 5   The risk and potential

At first need to create a plan. A plan will inform you when exactly you need to stop your trade to cut losses or help to increase a situation. When you need to exit a new trade to now you should profit or maybe size down on a position. As with each industry, you always aim for a advantageous risk or reward rate of at the least 3: 1. Risk or reward ratio is usually determined through support and resistance outlines. It means that if people enter a new trade using a stock price tag of $6 and you also are able to risk a lack of $1, you should be sure the chart is placed up for any potential pay back of $3. This is a simple rule of thumb which My spouse and i govern every one of my trading.

Cutting loss

Cutting losses has become one of my major rules once i day industry. A great deal of traders won't cut losses simply because BELIEVE how the stock will rebound. When you are trading, never allow yourself to lose greater than you earn, and to do that, you should cut ones losses decisively. You possibly can always enter this market again once the chart set itself upwards, but you'll be able to never get back the money you might have just missing.

How to find out a strong resistance or perhaps support collection?

A solid support or maybe resistance collection is one which has been tested with the chart more often than not but by no means been productively broken away from. A strong distinctive line of support or maybe resistance usually gives a better and more accurate determine for risk or pay back because when the information goes near this collection, the group believes how the line will serve for the reason that support or maybe resistance once more and reply accordingly. This becomes an incredibly strong self-fulfilling prediction. It is also useful to note that in the event the chart breaks away from a strong distinctive line of support or maybe resistance, it will typically experience a strong move towards its large.

When exchanging a inventory, it is significant to check out both your daily and intraday chart to spot if a real line exists within the 3-6month moment frames. In the event it prevails, you need to respect that strong distinctive line of support/resistance while trading your intraday information and plan your risk versus pay back accordingly.

COMPLETE NUMBER PSYCHOLOGY

Paying focus on whole range marks in addition helps inside gauging danger versus reward for any trade. Many traders focus on whole greenback marks ($10. 00) or maybe half greenback marks ($10. 50) a lot more closely. One example is, if your stock currently is priced from $9. 64 intraday and trending larger, many professionals will believe that it can easily push to $10. 00 and purchase into this. Once your stock visits $10. 00, everybody are going to be thinking of taking earnings and market off. At this time, the $10. 00 level is acting as a psychological distinctive line of resistance. It is usually wise to focus on this full and 50 % dollar mark if you are trading and make ideas based down these numbers.

Chapter 6   Advice for day trading

In the last chapter of the eBook, I am going to provide you some of the advice for day trading success, which you may not know. They are equally important as every other information in this eBook because you need to avoid some of the mistakes I am going to point out as well as concentrate on some good things and facts I am going to mention in the next couple of paragraphs.

I would like this chapter to be about pointing you out the mistakes you can make in day trading that could keep you away from success and profit.

I believe I found seven big mistakes any day trader can make. I found this to be extremely useful because if you remember, I mentioned that only 1 out of 10 people who try to make money with day trading actually succeed. Do you know what does that actually mean? Your chances to fail are much bigger than to succeed.

Here, you can see 7 advices for a successful day trading.

1: Do not Over-analyzing

The problem people usually make in day trading is that they over-analyze the market to find a trend. This approach is often very wrong and there is a misconception among people that says "more complicated formula and algorithm you have, the better are the odds for making profit." That is simply not true. Yes, it is good to have a formula and algorithm you follow, but you cannot forget one of the most important rules in day trading. You buy when the market is going up and sell when the market is going down

2: Be patient to take your profits

Do you know why only 1 out of 10 people reach success in day trading? It is because 9 out of 10 people are greedy. I do not know how many times I mentioned this and I am not sure how many times I will say it again; Day trading success comes from consistency and taking small profits. It is not a get-rich-quick scheme and success is possible only if you are patient.

3: Know the limit of losses

If you recall, I have already mentioned that if you want to reach success in day trading, you need to be okay with losing money. That is not strange, not even to most successful day traders. They lose money, too. A lot! But they are successful because they know how to limit their losses.

It is of extreme importance to know when to exit a certain trade to save money. It is always better to lose $300 than $3000 because you stayed to long.

4: Sticking with the right market

I am sure that you are going to reach success with certain type of market. The question is whether you will tie yourself to the same market forever. You need to follow the market! YOU NEED TO BE THE MARKET!

Another important fact is that you need to be in the market that is moving because, as I repeatedly say, buy when the market goes up and sell when it goes down. From that, we can conclude that you need to be okay with changes and adapting on new markets constantly. Go where the money is, and money is never in the steady market.

5: Develop a trading strategy

If you think you can succeed in today's world, in any profession, without a plan and a strategy, you are terribly wrong. No one can do that. That is the reason why I devoted a whole chapter to writing a successful trading strategy and its importance.

6: Control over yourself

When people describe me, they usually say that I am an incredibly calm person. This is because I learned how to control my emotions and my thoughts because if you do not control thoughts, they will control you.

Calmness should be the main characteristic of every successful trader. If you do not how to control your greediness, your fear or your panic, you will never succeed.

7: Do not Overtrading

Finally yet importantly, learn when it is enough. I think I talked about this on every seminar I had about day trading. Overtrading is the common problem of every day trader. When you reach your weekly goals, just stop! There is no reason to keep trading if you already made the profit you want.

People usually make these seven mistakes. I know you need to avoid them if you want profit. Now I am going to list some of the characteristics of successful day traders. Pay attention if you want to develop some serious skills.

They do not blame other people because of their losses and failures. They think that is normal and there is no reason to blame your broker or any other person because you lost money on certain trade.

They have a system. In the system, they developed every possible situation that can happen. They do not stay in the losing trade and they do not hurry and rush into trades. They are precise, they take their time and they are well aware of each step they make. That is why they are successful.

They learned how to adapt. Maybe I didn't stress out how this is important in day trading because market constantly changes and if you want to keep having profits, you need to go with the change.

Conclusion

Thank you again for downloading this book!

I hope this book was able to help you to understand about how to day trade.

I hope you absorbed all the information in this eBook because you are going to need it. I am sure you are going to remember the most important facts because I was pointing them out constantly. You may not know how they are important now, but you will definitely remember what I was saying once when you start trading.

Finally, if you enjoyed this book, then I'd like to ask you for a favor, would you be kind enough to leave a review for this book on Amazon? It'd be greatly appreciated!

Thank you and good luck!

www.ingramcontent.com/pod-product-compliance
Lightning Source LLC
Chambersburg PA
CBHW072312200526
45168CB00014B/1414